The Power of Innerstanding

Breaking Free From The Matrix

By: Lori Ann Gros

Mamee

Dedication Page

This book is dedicated to the creator and every individual striving to break free from limiting beliefs, rewrite their story, and create a life of wealth, abundance, and fulfillment.

To those who dare to dream, manifest, and rise — this is for you.

Copyright Page

Copyright © 2025 Lori Ann Gros (Mamee)

All rights reserved.

Author - Lori Ann Gros (Mamee)

Publisher- Mamee' Magic Press

mameemagicpress@gmail.com

Facebook Lori Mamee Gros

ISBN: 979830954145

First Edition, 2025

Table of Contents

Chapter 1: The Matrix of Beliefs Breaking Free from the Mental Prison

Chapter 2: Gratitude — The Wealth Magnet

Chapter 3: The Universal Laws

Chapter 4: Karma — The Cycle of Energy Return

Chapter 5: The Wealth Mindset

Chapter 6: Breaking Free from the Matrix

Chapter 7: Manifestation Methods and Exercises

Chapter 8: Financial Freedom Blueprint

Chapter 9: Sustaining a High Vibration Life

Chapter 10: Final Reflection and Next Steps

Chapter 1:
The Matrix of Beliefs
Breaking Free from the Mental Prison

Imagine waking up one day and realizing that the life you're living—the job you have, the way you manage money, the relationships you nurture—was largely programmed by the environment you grew up in. From childhood, society, family, and culture have shaped your beliefs about what is possible, how much money you can earn, and even what kind of person you think you should be.

This system of thoughts and conditioning is what many call "the matrix." It's an invisible cage designed to keep people in patterns of limitation and survival. But the good news is: you have the power to break free.

The Program You're Living In

Every thought you think emits a frequency. These thoughts shape your emotions, which dictate your actions, and ultimately create your reality. Most people live on autopilot, unaware that they are repeating old patterns that were programmed into their subconscious mind before they were even old enough to question them.

Society encourages this cycle by feeding fear, scarcity, and the belief that wealth, happiness, and freedom are reserved for the few. From "money doesn't grow on trees" to "you have to work hard to succeed," these beliefs are ingrained early and reinforced throughout life.

But none of it is inherently true.

Redefining Your Beliefs

To break free from the matrix, you must first identify the beliefs that are keeping you trapped. Ask yourself:

What do I believe about money?

What do I believe about success?

Do I feel worthy of abundance?

| |
| |
| |

Who told me I couldn't have it all?

| |
| |
| |

Most of your limiting beliefs didn't come from you—they came from someone else. Once you recognize this, you gain the power to rewrite your mental programming.

Journal Prompt

"Write down three limiting beliefs you currently hold about money, success, or happiness. Where did these beliefs come from? How do they show up in your daily life?"

Reprogramming the Mind

The next step is to replace these limiting beliefs with empowering ones. Instead of "money is hard to come by," affirm: "Money flows to me effortlessly and abundantly." Instead of "I have to work hard to be successful," say, "I align with inspired action and attract success with ease."

It's not just about saying the words—
it's about feeling the truth of them.
When you start reprogramming your
thoughts, your mind will resist. It will
tell you that it's not possible, that
you're being unrealistic. But with
repetition and practice, you will shift
your vibration to one that matches
abundance and freedom.

Exercise: Thought Audit

Write down five recurring negative
thoughts you have throughout the
day.

Beside each thought, write a positive affirmation to counter it.

Repeat these affirmations daily, especially when the negative thoughts arise.

Breaking the Loop

The matrix thrives on routine and predictability. To truly break free, you must do things differently. Start by disrupting your daily patterns:

Change your morning routine.

Learn something new.

Step outside your comfort zone.

These small shifts signal to your subconscious that you're ready for transformation.

Affirmation for Freedom:

"I am the master of my mind. I release old limitations and step into infinite possibilities."

Final Reflection

The matrix isn't a physical place—it's a mental construct. And as powerful as it may seem, it has no control over you unless you give it permission. When you begin questioning your beliefs and intentionally choosing new ones, you reclaim your power.

By the end of this chapter, you've already taken the first step toward freedom: Awareness

Now it's time to continue your journey toward the life you were truly meant to live.

Chapter 2

Gratitude — The Wealth Magnet

Unlocking the Power of Appreciation

Gratitude is more than just saying "thank you" when something good happens. It's a powerful energetic frequency that aligns you with abundance. When you practice gratitude, you shift your focus from what's lacking to what's already present and beautiful in your life. This simple shift can change everything.

Most people fall into the trap of waiting for big breakthroughs or material success before they feel grateful. But here's the truth: the universe responds to the energy you emit right now. If you're constantly focused on scarcity, frustration, or dissatisfaction, you're only attracting more of the same.

However, when you cultivate genuine appreciation for the present moment—even the smallest blessings—you naturally magnetize greater abundance and success into your life.

How Gratitude Shifts Your Energy

Every thought and feeling sends out a vibration. Negative emotions such as fear, envy, or doubt vibrate at lower frequencies, while gratitude and joy vibrate at some of the highest frequencies.

Think of your thoughts and emotions as signals you're sending to the universe. When you're grateful, you're essentially saying: "I'm ready to receive more of this goodness." The universe responds by delivering more things for you to be grateful for.

This isn't just a spiritual idea—it's backed by science. Studies have shown that people who practice gratitude regularly experience greater happiness, improved relationships, and even better physical health.

Gratitude in Action: Small Shifts, Big Rewards

You don't need extravagant reasons to be thankful. Start with the basics:

The air you're breathing right now

A meal that nourished your body

A kind word from a friend or stranger

The more you notice and appreciate these simple things, the more your life will begin to overflow with abundance.

Journal Prompt

"List 10 things you're grateful for right now, no matter how small or simple they may seem. Write why each one matters to you."

Daily Gratitude Practice

Make gratitude part of your daily routine. Here's a simple practice you can use:

1. **Morning Gratitude:** Before getting out of bed, think of three things you're grateful for.

2. **Evening Reflection:** Write down five positive things that happened during the day, even if they seemed insignificant.

Gratitude Letter: Write a letter to someone who has impacted your life positively, even if you don't plan to send it.

Exercise: Gratitude Amplifier

For one week, commit to this practice:

1. Each morning, spend 5 minutes visualizing the life of your dreams as if it has already happened. Feel deep gratitude for it.

2. Throughout the day, mentally say "thank you" whenever something good happens, no matter how small.

3. At night, write in your journal: "Thank you for ___." Fill in the blank with three things.

| |
| |
| |
| |

Gratitude and Financial Abundance

One of the biggest blocks to wealth is resentment or dissatisfaction around money. You may find yourself thinking things like:

"I never have enough money."

"Why do others have more than me?"

These thoughts create resistance and block the flow of financial abundance. Instead, try this shift:

"I'm grateful for every dollar that comes into my life."

"Money flows to me easily, and I use it wisely."

Even if you're struggling financially, find something to appreciate—whether it's the ability to buy groceries, pay a bill, or the potential to create more wealth.

Affirmation for Abundance:

"I am grateful for all that I have and all that is on its way to me. I am a magnet for wealth, success, and joy."

Final Reflection

Gratitude is the gateway to receiving more in life. It transforms what you have into enough and opens the doors for greater abundance. By making it a daily practice, you not only change your thoughts—you change your entire energetic vibration.

The universe Is always listening. Speak the language of appreciation, and watch as miracles unfold.

Chapter 3: The Universal Laws

Mastering the Blueprint of Reality

There's a powerful framework that governs every aspect of life—whether or not you're aware of it. These principles are known as the universal laws. Like gravity, they're always at work, shaping your experiences, thoughts, and outcomes.

Understanding and aligning with these laws can radically transform your life. Instead of struggling against the current, you begin to flow effortlessly toward abundance, success, and happiness.

This chapter will introduce you to the most transformative universal laws and show you how to harness them to create the life of your dreams.

The Law of Attraction: Like Attracts Like

The Law of Attraction is one of the most well-known universal laws. It states that whatever you focus on with intention and emotion will be drawn into your life.

If you constantly think about lack, struggle, or fear, you'll attract more of those experiences. On the other hand, when you focus on abundance, joy, and success, you naturally magnetize those things toward you.

But it's not just about thinking positively— it's about embodying the feelings of already having what you desire.

Journal Prompt:

"What do I want to attract into my life? How would I feel if I already had it?"

Exercise:

Close your eyes and visualize your ideal life.

See yourself living it fully—where are you, who are you with, and how does it feel?

Spend 5 minutes a day immersing yourself in this visualization.

The Law of Vibration: Energy is Everything

At the core of the universe is energy, and everything vibrates at a specific frequency— including your thoughts, emotions, and beliefs.

When your vibration is low (filled with doubt, fear, or frustration), it becomes difficult to attract positive experiences. When you raise your vibration through joy, gratitude, and love, you naturally align with higher opportunities and outcomes.

How to Raise Your Vibration:

Practice gratitude daily

Surround yourself with uplifting people Meditate and focus on positive emotions

Affirmation for High Vibration:

"I radiate joy, abundance, and love. My energy attracts limitless opportunities."

The Law of Cause and Effect: Karma

Every action you take sends out energy that returns to you in some form. This is often referred to as karma.

Karma isn't punishment or reward—it's simply the universe reflecting your energy back to you. Positive actions and intentions lead to positive outcomes, while negative energy invites challenges.

Exercise:

Reflect on past actions that may have created negative patterns in your life.

Write down three ways you can start putting out positive energy today.

For each action, state an intention: "I choose to give love, kindness, and abundance without expectation."

The Law of Inspired Action: Move Toward Your Goals

Manifestation isn't just about thinking positive thoughts—it's about taking action when inspired.

When you set intentions and align with your desires, the universe will present opportunities. Your job is to recognize these signs and act on them.

Journal Prompt:

"What is one step I can take today, no matter how small, that moves me closer to my goal?"

The Law of Detachment: Let Go to Receive

This law teaches that you must release attachment to specific outcomes in order to manifest your desires. When you cling to how something "must" happen, you create resistance.

Trust that the universe knows the best way to bring your desires to you, even if it looks different from what you imagined.

Affirmation for Trust:

"I release control and trust that everything is working out for my highest good."

Applying the Universal Laws

To truly benefit from these laws, practice the following steps:

1. **Set a Clear Intention:** Know what you want and why.

2. **Align Your Vibration:** Feel the emotions of already having it.

3. **Take Inspired Action:** Move toward your goals confidently.

4. **Let Go and Trust:** Release any need for control.

Affirmation for Alignment:

"I align with the universal laws. My thoughts, feelings, and actions create limitless abundance."

Final Reflection

The universe is not random—it's precise, intentional, and responsive. When you understand its laws and learn to work with them instead of against them, you become the conscious creator of your life.

Mastering these principles will unlock the door to limitless potential. You already have the power within you—now it's time to wield it.

Chapter 4
Karma — The Cycle of Energy Return

What You Give Out, You Get Back

Karma is often misunderstood. Many people think of it as a form of cosmic punishment or reward — a kind of universal scorecard keeping track of good and bad deeds. But karma is far more profound than that. At its core, karma is simply the law of cause and effect: every action, thought, and intention sends out energy that inevitably comes back to you.

What you put into the world—whether love, kindness, anger, or greed—has a ripple effect that shapes your experiences. Understanding this truth empowers you to consciously direct your energy in a way that creates the life you desire.

The Energetic Boomerang

Imagine throwing a boomerang into the air. The energy and direction you give it determine where and how it returns to you. Life works the same way.

If you spread love and positivity, those energies will find their way back to you.

If you emit fear, resentment, or selfishness, you'll attract situations that mirror those vibrations.

Karma doesn't operate on a fixed timeline. Sometimes the return is immediate, and other times it unfolds over months or even years. But rest assured, the energy always finds its way back.

Breaking Negative Cycles

If you feel stuck in patterns of struggle or disappointment, it might be time to examine your karmic energy.

Ask yourself:

Am I holding onto resentment or anger toward someone?

Do I give without expecting anything in return?

How can I be a source of light and positivity for others?

The key to breaking negative karmic loops is forgiveness—both for yourself and others.
Letting go doesn't mean condoning harmful behavior; it means freeing

yourself from the chains of negative energy.

Journal Prompt

"Write about a situation where you felt wronged. How can you release the negative energy surrounding this experience? What lessons did it teach you?"

Exercise: Clearing Karma Through Forgiveness

1. Sit quietly and close your eyes.

2. Bring to mind someone you need to forgive—even if it's yourself.

3. Say silently or out loud:

"I release you and this situation from my heart. I choose peace and forgiveness. May both of us find healing and happiness." Repeat this practice daily until you feel lighter and free from resentment.

Creating Positive Karma

Building good karma is simple but requires intentional effort.

Here are a few ways to start:

Practice Kindness: Offer compliments, help someone in need, or simply listen with compassion.

Be Generous: Give without expecting anything in return.

Live with Integrity: Keep your promises and honor your word.

When you align your actions with positive intentions, you naturally attract more joy and abundance into your life.

Affirmation for Positive Karma:

"I give love, kindness, and positivity to the world, and these energies return to me multiplied."

Final Reflection

Karma is not about judgment—it's about balance. By choosing thoughts and actions rooted in love, compassion, and generosity, you become the architect of your destiny.

The universe Is always watching, not to punish, but to mirror back the energy you project. Choose wisely, and watch as your life transforms in extraordinary ways.

Chapter 5

The Wealth Mindset

Rewiring Your Mind for Abundance

If you want to be wealthy, you must first think like someone who already is. Wealth begins in the mind long before it manifests in your bank account. The beliefs, thoughts, and emotions you hold about money directly shape your financial reality.

Most people are trapped in a scarcity mindset—believing there's never enough money, that making money is hard, or that wealth is reserved for a lucky few. These limiting beliefs keep them stuck in financial struggle. But when you shift your perspective and develop a mindset rooted in abundance, you unlock the ability to create lasting financial success and generational wealth.

What Is a Wealth Mindset?

A wealth mindset is the belief that financial success is possible for you and that there is more than enough to go around. It involves thinking creatively, taking inspired action, and viewing money as a tool to create freedom, impact, and joy.

People with a wealth mindset:

See opportunities where others see obstacles

Take calculated risks

Believe in their ability to create financial success

Practice gratitude for what they have

Identifying Limiting Beliefs

To rewire your mind for wealth, you must first identify the negative beliefs holding you back.

Ask yourself:

What did I learn about money growing up?

Do I believe I'm worthy of financial success?

What fears do I have about becoming wealthy?

Write down your answers and be honest. These beliefs likely came from parents, society, or past experiences—but they do not define your future.

Journal Prompt

"What are three limiting beliefs I hold about money? How have these beliefs affected my financial decisions?"

Reprogramming Your Wealth Blueprint

Now that you've identified your limiting beliefs, it's time to replace them with empowering thoughts.

Here's how:

1. **Affirmations:** Create statements that reflect the financial reality you want to manifest.

Example: "I am worthy of unlimited wealth.
Money flows to me effortlessly."

2. **Visualization:** Spend 5-10 minutes daily visualizing yourself living your dream financial life. See yourself paying bills with ease, investing wisely, and enjoying the freedom wealth brings.

3. **Gratitude:** Focus on appreciating the money you currently have, no matter how small.

Exercise: Wealth Manifestation Ritual

1. Write down your top three financial goals.

2. For each goal, write why you want it and how achieving it will feel.

3. Each morning, read your goals aloud and visualize yourself achieving them.

| |
| |
| |

Generational Wealth: Creating a Legacy

True financial success isn't just about accumulating wealth—it's about creating a lasting legacy for future generations. This involves wise investing, financial education, and breaking toxic financial patterns.

Steps to build generational wealth:

Invest Wisely: Learn about real estate, stocks, and other assets that grow over time.

Teach Financial Literacy: Educate your children and loved ones about money management.

Create Multiple Streams of Income: Don't rely solely on one source of income.

Affirmation for Wealth:

"I am a magnet for abundance. Wealth flows to me, and I use it wisely to create a legacy."

Final Reflection

The wealth mindset isn't just about thinking positively—it's about aligning your thoughts, emotions, and actions with financial success. By breaking free from limiting beliefs and adopting new empowering habits, you pave the way for unlimited prosperity.

The journey to financial freedom begins in your mind. Own it, believe it, and watch as your life transforms.

Chapter 6

Breaking Free from the Matrix Living Life on Your Terms

The "matrix" is the system of societal programming that keeps people trapped in conformity, scarcity, and limitation. It's the invisible force that tells you to work a 9-to-5 job, follow a predictable path, and settle for less than you desire.

Breaking free from the matrix requires courage, awareness, and a willingness to challenge the status quo. It's about reclaiming your power and living life on your terms.

The Illusion of Security

Society teaches you to seek security in jobs, relationships, and routines. But true security doesn't come from external sources—it comes from within.

When you realize that you are the creator of your reality, you no longer need to rely on external systems for validation or success. You become empowered to design a life that aligns with your deepest desires.

Steps to Break Free from the Matrix

1. Question Everything:

Why do I believe what I believe?

Who benefits from my staying in this system?

2. Trust Your Inner Voice:

Your intuition is your greatest guide. When something feels off, listen.

3. Take Bold Action:

Stepping outside the matrix requires courage. Pursue your dreams even when others doubt you.

4. Create Financial Freedom:

Build multiple streams of income and invest in your own growth. Financial independence is key to breaking free.

Journal Prompt

"What would my ideal life look like if I had no limitations? What steps can I take to move toward that vision?"

Affirmation for Freedom:

"I am free to create the life I desire. I trust my intuition and follow my path boldly."

Final Reflection

Breaking free from the matrix is a journey of self-discovery and empowerment. By questioning societal norms and trusting yourself, you step into a life of authenticity, freedom, and limitless potential.

Chapter 7

Gratitude in Action

Living a Life of Appreciation

Gratitude is not just a fleeting feeling—it's a way of life. When practiced consistently, it becomes a powerful force that transforms your thoughts, emotions, and circumstances.

By actively practicing gratitude, you unlock new levels of happiness, attract greater abundance, and cultivate a mindset that naturally supports success. This chapter will guide you on how to put gratitude into action daily so that it becomes a driving force in your life.

The Ripple Effect of Gratitude

When you express gratitude, you emit positive energy that affects not only yourself but those around you. It strengthens relationships, opens doors to new opportunities, and creates an atmosphere where abundance can thrive.

Gratitude is contagious—when you embody it, others naturally feel uplifted and inspired by your presence.

Simple Ways to Live Gratefully

1. Morning Gratitude Ritual:

Upon waking, list three things you're thankful for before getting out of bed.

2. Gratitude Walks:

Take a walk outdoors and mentally note everything you're grateful for, from the fresh air to the beauty of nature.

3. Gratitude Jar:

Write down one thing you're grateful for each day and place it in a jar. Over time, this becomes a visual reminder of your blessings.

4. Verbal Appreciation:

Tell people how much you appreciate them.

Journal Exercise: The Gratitude Letter

Write a letter to someone who has made a positive impact on your life. Share specific ways they have helped you and express your genuine appreciation. Whether you send it or not, this exercise will uplift your spirit.

Transforming Challenges with Gratitude

Even difficult situations hold hidden blessings. When faced with a challenge, ask yourself:

What can I learn from this experience?

How has this situation helped me grow?

Finding the silver lining in adversity builds resilience and strengthens your belief that life is always working in your favor.

Affirmation for Gratitude:

"I am grateful for every experience, knowing that each one brings growth, wisdom, and abundance."

Final Reflection

Gratitude is the gateway to joy and prosperity. By choosing to live in appreciation, you align yourself with the abundant flow of the universe. Practice it daily, and watch as your life blossoms in unimaginable ways.

Chapter 8
Living in Alignment with Universal Laws

Becoming a Co-Creator of Your Reality

Mastering the universal laws allows you to live as a conscious creator of your life. When you align your thoughts, emotions, and actions with these principles, you unlock your full potential and experience success, joy, and fulfillment on a grand scale.

This chapter will help you integrate the universal laws into your everyday life so they become second nature.

Daily Practices for Alignment

1. Mindful Intention Setting:

Start each day by setting a clear intention for how you want to feel and what you want to achieve.

2. Emotional Mastery:

Monitor your emotional state throughout the day. If you find yourself slipping into negative thoughts, pause and reset your vibration through deep breaths or positive affirmations.

3. Inspired Action:

Pay attention to intuitive nudges and act on them without hesitation.

4. Trust and Surrender:

Release attachment to how things "should" happen. Trust that the universe has your back.

Exercise: Visualization Power Hour

1. Spend 10 minutes visualizing your ideal life.

2. Focus on how it feels to already have everything you desire.

3. Write down any ideas or inspired actions that come to mind during this time.

Affirmation for Alignment:

"I am perfectly aligned with the abundant flow of the universe. My thoughts, actions, and energy create limitless success."

Final Reflection

Living in alignment with universal laws turns life into an exciting adventure where miracles and opportunities are always within reach. Embrace these principles and watch your reality transform.

Chapter 9

Designing Your Dream Life

Creating a Vision and Taking Action

It's time to put everything you've learned into practice by designing the life of your dreams. This chapter will guide you in setting powerful goals, creating a vision, and mapping out actionable steps to bring your desires to life.

Step 1: Define Your Dream Life

Ask yourself:

What does my ideal day look like?

Who am I surrounded by?

How do I feel emotionally, physically, and spiritually?

Write down your answers in vivid detail.

Step 2: Set SMART Goals

Your goals should be:

Specific: Clearly define what you want.

Measurable: Track your progress.

Achievable: Set realistic expectations.

Relevant: Align with your purpose.

Time-bound: Assign deadlines.

Example: "I will save $50,000 for my dream home within the next two years by investing and budgeting wisely."

Step 3: Create a Vision Board

Collect images and words that represent your goals and place them where you'll see them daily.

Step 4: Take Inspired Action

Break your goals down into manageable steps and commit to taking at least one action daily.

Affirmation for Success:

"I am the creator of my reality. Every day, I take inspired action toward my dreams."

Final Reflection

Your dream life is within reach. By setting a clear vision, taking intentional action, and trusting the process, you step into a future filled with abundance, joy, and fulfillment.

Conclusion: The Journey Begins Now

You hold the power to transform your life. By mastering your thoughts, practicing gratitude, understanding karma, and living in alignment with universal laws, you become the conscious creator of your reality.

Remember:

You are worthy of wealth, love, and joy.

What you focus on expands.

Gratitude unlocks infinite possibilities.

Affirmation to Close:

"I am limitless. I am abundant. I am grateful.
My dreams are already coming true."

Acknowledgments

First and foremost, I give gratitude to the Creator for guiding me through the journey of writing this book. Thank you for the divine wisdom and inspiration that allowed this message to flow through me.

To my family and friends, your unwavering support, love, and belief in my vision have kept me motivated throughout this journey. Your words of encouragement carried me during moments of doubt, and your presence reminded me of the power of connection and love.

To every reader of The Power of Innerstanding , I honor you for seeking to unlock your highest potential and break free from limiting beliefs. Your courage and determination to transform your life inspire me deeply.

A special thanks to everyone who shared wisdom, insights, or energy that contributed to the pages of this book. You are all lights on this path of awakening.

Lastly, to my readers: this book exists because of your hunger for knowledge, growth, and abundance. Thank you for allowing me to be part of your transformative journey.

— Lori Ann Gros (Mamee)

Author's Biography

Lori Ann Gros, affectionately known as "Mamee," is a passionate thought leader, author, and spiritual guide dedicated to helping individuals break free from limiting beliefs and align with their highest potential. With a profound understanding of universal laws and the dynamics of the "matrix" that shapes everyday experiences, Mamee empowers readers to rewrite their stories, embrace abundance, and create lives filled with purpose, wealth, and joy.

Drawing from personal experiences, spiritual practices, and years of self-mastery, Lori Ann provides practical tools and transformative insights for manifesting success and fulfillment. Her message is simple yet powerful: you are the creator of your own reality, and with the right mindset, anything is possible.

When she's not writing or teaching, Mamee enjoys connecting with nature, practicing gratitude, and inspiring others to live fully and authentically.

Keep this book close. Use it as a guide, a journal, and a source of inspiration as you continue your journey. Your best life is waiting for you—go out and claim it.

Made in the USA
Columbia, SC
02 March 2025